D1305670

TOOLS FOR TEACHERS

- **ATOS:** 0.9
- **GRL:** D
- **LEXILE:** 280L
- **CURRICULUM CONNECTIONS:** community helpers
- **WORD COUNT:** 95

Skills to Teach

- **HIGH-FREQUENCY WORDS:** a, have, he, I, in, it, me, my, of, on, she, the, who
- **CONTENT WORDS:** bandage, bone, cast, dad, dentist, doctor, filling, heart, medicine, mom, nurse, surgeon, temperature, tooth
- **PUNCTUATION:** periods, question mark, exclamation point
- **WORD STUDY:** short /e/, spelled ea (healthy); r-controlled vowels (doctor, heart, nurse, surgeon); long /oo/, spelled ou (soup); three-syllable words (medicine, operates); four-syllable word (temperature); /n/, spelled kn (knee)
- **TEXT TYPE:** information report

Before Reading Activities

- Read the title and give a simple statement of the main idea.
- Have students "walk" though the book and talk about what they see in the pictures.
- Introduce new vocabulary by having students predict the first letter and locate the word in the text.
- Discuss any unfamiliar concepts that are in the text.

After Reading Activities

Encourage children to talk about the people in the book who help keep them healthy. Which of these community helpers have they met before, and what kind of experience did they have with each? Do they know anyone who works as a dentist, doctor, nurse, or surgeon? Who else do they know who helps keep them healthy?

Tadpole Books are published by Jump!, 5357 Penn Avenue South, Minneapolis, MN 55419, www.jumplibrary.com

Editor: Jenny Fretland VanVoorst **Designer:** Anna Peterson

Photo Credits: Dreamstime: Liudmyla Boichenko, 8–9; Getty: asiseeit, 4–5; Caiaimage/Robert Daly, 12–13; Portra Images, 12–13. iStock: IPGGutenberg UKLtd, 10–11. Shutterstock: Zerbor, cover; MOHD HAIRUBIN BRAHIM, 1; Photographee.eu, 2–3; adriaticfoto, 6–7; Monkey Business Images, 14–15.
Library of Congress Cataloging-in-Publication Data is available at www.loc.gov or upon request from the publisher.
ISBN: 978-1-62031-761-7 (hardcover)
ISBN: 978-1-62031-781-5 (paperback)
ISBN: 978-1-62496-608-8 (ebook)

WHO HELPS KEEP US HEALTHY?

by Erica Donner

TABLE OF CONTENTS

tadpole
books

WHO HELPS KEEP US HEALTHY?

I have a cold.

My mom feeds me soup. She puts me to bed.

3

My arm is broken.

A doctor sets the bone. She puts it in a cast.

5

I have a fever.

A nurse takes my temperature. He gives me medicine.

My tooth hurts.

A dentist cleans it out. He puts in a filling.

bandage

I hurt my knee.

My dad cleans
the cut. He puts
on a bandage.

11

I have a heart problem.

surgeon

A surgeon operates. He fixes the damaged part.

Who helps keep us healthy?

Lots of people!

WORDS TO KNOW

dad

dentist

doctor

mom

nurse

surgeon

INDEX